UNLOCKING DIVINE JUSTICE

Unlocking Divine Justice

Navigating the Courts of Heaven

Bill Vincent

ArcanaVerse Books

CONTENTS

"I've transformed my sermons into book form. Please note that we've refined the content for clarity and a smoother reading experience. We trust you'll find it engaging."

1

UNLOCKING DIVINE JUSTICE: NAVIGATING THE COURTS OF HEAVEN

I aim to share insights that will truly empower you, guiding you to the fulfillment that God has planned for you. Jesus's teachings on prayer, as chronicled in the Gospels, reveal a multifaceted understanding of communication with the divine. You'll find that in Matthew and Mark, for instance, prayer is depicted in various forms and concepts, from Jesus praying throughout the night to his early morning devotions. In John, you'll encounter foundational principles of prayer. However, it's in Luke's account that Jesus's teachings on prayer truly flourish, offering vivid portrayals of prayer that help us grasp what transpires in the spiritual realm when we pray.

One profound shift in my understanding came when I began to comprehend the Courts of Heaven. My perspective of the spiritual realm transformed from viewing it as a battlefield to recognizing it as a courtroom. This distinction is crucial; mistaking a courtroom for a battlefield can lead us to adopt the wrong strategies in our spiritual endeavors. Have your prayers seemed unanswered for a prolonged period? Often, we attribute this to personal shortcomings, a lack of faith, or perceive it as not aligning with God's timing. However, consider the possibility that something in the spiritual legal system might be hindering God's response to your prayers.

Understanding this necessitates a discussion about dimensions, particularly as Jesus addresses them in Luke 11 and 18. Jesus introduces the concept of approaching God as a Father, emphasizing the importance of this perception. Yet, many believers struggle with this due to past negative experiences or misconceptions about fatherhood. Only through the 'Spirit of Adoption' can we truly embrace God as our Father, experiencing both His endearing love and authoritative guidance. This duality is essential; focusing solely on God's love without recognizing His authority can lead to lawlessness, while an exclusive focus on His authority may breed legalism.

Furthermore, Jesus elucidates another dimension of our relationship with God – that of friendship. This dynamic is distinct from the paternal relationship and involves sharing confidences and understanding God's will and intentions. This aspect of our relationship with God empowers us to intercede and act in matters beyond our personal sphere, influencing even national and global issues.

The narrative then shifts to a discussion on communal and spiritual responsibilities, emphasizing the Church's role in the spiritual realm. The Church is not just a collection of individuals but holds a recognized position in heaven, entrusted with the responsibility to address and influence matters that extend beyond personal needs to national and global concerns.

In conclusion, Jesus's teachings on prayer introduce us to multiple dimensions of our relationship with God – as our Father, as our friend, and as a judge in the spiritual court-room. Understanding and navigating these dimensions can profoundly impact not only our personal lives but also the broader world, aligning us more closely with God's will and purposes.

Let's delve deeper into these three dimensions of spiri-tual intercession. It's imperative to clarify that the parable of the widow and the unjust judge isn't meant to depict God as reluctant or unjust but to highlight the power of persistent faith. If a widow could obtain justice from a cor-rupt judge, imagine how much more we, as God's chosen, can receive from the ultimate Righteous Judge. This nar-rative serves as a profound reminder of God's unwavering commitment to justice for His people.

Now, consider these three pivotal aspects. Jesus's teach-ings about approaching God as Father encompass our per-sonal needs – our sustenance and well-being, akin to a father providing bread, fish, and eggs for his children. In this role, God meets our individual needs, reflecting the nurturing aspect of His nature. As earthly fathers naturally respond to their children's needs, our Heavenly Father is attuned to our prayers for provision and support.

However, our relationship with God transcends paternal bonds. When we intercede for others, we step into a role of spiritual intercession, akin to a friend helping another friend in need. This reflects Jesus's teaching about a friend who, unable to meet another friend's need, seeks assistance from a third party. This middle position, one of intercession, highlights our role in appealing to God on behalf of others, echoing the intercessory acts of biblical figures like Abraham and Moses.

The third dimension involves approaching God as Judge, especially when confronting adversity. This is not about engaging in a battlefield scenario but stepping into a courtroom setting. This distinction is crucial; Jesus's teachings and the vivid imagery of Revelation 19:11 emphasize the judicial aspect of divine intervention. It's a powerful reminder that true victory over adversaries comes from legal triumph in the heavenly court, not merely on earthly battlegrounds.

Understanding the adversary's tactics is vital. The term 'adversary' in the spiritual context signifies a legal opponent, one who brings accusations in a divine court of law. This perspective is pivotal in comprehending the spiritual battles we face. The enemy's power lies in legal accusations, seeking to deny us our rightful blessings. Recognizing this legal dimension shifts our spiritual strategy from mere confrontation to seeking divine justice.

Acknowledging this, we must discern the legal grounds that the adversary might exploit. Scripture highlights three primary areas: sin, transgression, and iniquity, each representing different facets of spiritual breaches. Sin, often understood as missing the mark, can include wrong motives, as seen in the case of Job. Transgression speaks of willful defiance or crossing a moral boundary. Iniquity, perhaps the most profound, refers to deep-seated corruption, often passed down generations, influencing our identity, choices, and destiny.

The battle against iniquity is not just personal; it's generational. It's about confronting and rectifying the deep-rooted issues within our bloodlines that deviate us from our God-ordained paths. The redemption from iniquity not only releases us from the adversary's legal claims but also realigns us with our divine purpose.

In summary, understanding these three dimensions – approaching God as Father, as Friend, and as Judge – equips us with a comprehensive strategy for spiritual warfare. It's not just about confronting the enemy but about understanding and rectifying the legal grounds in the spiritual realm that may hinder our prayers and destiny. This understanding transforms our spiritual walk, leading us from a place of struggle to a position of divine authority and victory.

David, long reigning as king, faced a dire situation. Due to a broken covenant, an adversary was granted legal grounds to inflict a three-year famine on the land. To lift this affliction, David was instructed to address the historical breach – the covenant Saul had violated. Upon rectifying this broken covenant, a significant shift occurred: the Bible states that God heeded the prayers for the land, marking a swift response after a prolonged period of unanswered prayers. This underscores a crucial spiritual principle: addressing the legal obstacles can unlock divine intervention and bring about immediate answers to longstanding prayers.

In the spiritual realm, altars and sacrifices hold profound significance, their utterances creating portals, some of which may be demonic, casting shadows like depression over individuals and their lineage. To truly liberate someone, it's not just about repentance; it involves dismantling the problematic altar, silencing the sacrifice that speaks through it, and sealing the opened portal. When these steps are taken, there's a palpable shift in the spiritual atmosphere, setting the stage for freedom and deliverance.

In a spirit of gratitude, we acknowledge our Heavenly Father – our Abba – who not only provides for our needs but also shares divine secrets, enabling us to enact change even in the spiritual realms. We cherish this bond, recognizing the ultimate legal transaction in history: the sacrifice of Jesus on the cross. It's through this profound act that we can approach God as Judge, clothed in righteousness, seeking to address any accusations the adversary might levy against us or our families.

In humility, we repent for any sin, misguided motives, or acts of rebellion, asking for cleansing and redemption through the powerful blood of Jesus. We seek to nullify any accusations, ensuring our offerings and intentions are pure and righteous, thereby dismantling any legal grounds the adversary might claim. As we engage in this spiritual process, we invite the liberating presence of God to permeate our lives, declaring the liberty of God to manifest fully and powerfully. Now and always!

ABOUT THE AUTHOR

Diving deep into the realms of spiritual awakening, Bill Vincent embodies a connection with the Supernatural that spans over three decades. With a robust prophetic anointing, he has dedicated his life to ministry, serving as a guiding light and a pillar of strength in Revival Waves of Glory Ministries.

Bill Vincent is not just a Minister but a prolific Author, contributing to the spiritual enlightenment of many through his diverse range of writings and teachings. His work encompasses themes of deliverance, fostering the presence of God, and shaping Apostolic, cutting-edge Church structure. His insights are drawn from a wellspring of experience, steeped in Revival, and fine-tuned by a profound Spiritual Sensitivity.

In his relentless pursuit of God's Presence and his commitment to sustaining Revival, Bill focuses primarily on inviting divine encounters and maintaining a spiritual atmosphere ripe for transformation. His extensive library of over 125 books serves as a beacon of hope, guiding countless individuals in overcoming the shackles of Satan and embracing the light of God.

Revival Waves of Glory Ministries is not your typical church – it's a prophetic ministry, a sanctuary where the Holy Spirit is given the freedom to move as He wills. Our sermons, a blend of divine wisdom and revelation, can be experienced on Rumble, immersing you in the transformative power of the Word: https://rumble.com/c/revivalwavesof-gloryministriesbillvincent

For a deeper exploration into our teachings, visions, and the manifold grace of God, visit https://www.revival-wavesofgloryministries.com/.

Embark on a journey of spiritual discovery with Bill Vincent, and let the waves of revival wash over you, unveiling the divine power and boundless love of God!

Podcast: https://podcasters.spotify.com/pod/show/bill-vincent2

Rumble: https://rumble.com/c/revivalwavesofglorymin-istriesbillvincent

Be sure to check out our new videos **Downloads From Heaven!**

REVIEW BY JIM STEPHENS

"Unlocking Divine Justice: Navigating the Courts of Heaven" is a profoundly insightful and transformative guide for anyone looking to deepen their spiritual journey. The author masterfully unravels the complex dynamics of the spiritual realm, presenting the reader with a compelling narrative that is both biblically grounded and immensely practical.

The book's exploration of the three pivotal dimensions of approaching God – as Father, Friend, and Judge – is not only enlightening but also offers a fresh perspective on prayer and spiritual warfare. The author's ability to weave scriptural references with real-life applications is commendable, making the principles within the book accessible and actionable.

What sets this book apart is its in-depth discussion of the legal framework of the spiritual realm. The concept that unresolved legal issues in the spiritual court can impede our prayers and blessings is a revelation, offering a new lens through which to understand challenges and blockages in one's spiritual life.

The guided prayers and actionable steps toward spiritual cleansing and dealing with generational issues are invaluable resources that empower the reader to confront and dismantle the adversary's legal grounds. This book doesn't just inform; it equips and empowers.

"Unlocking Divine Justice" is a treasure trove of spiritual wisdom, offering clarity, hope, and guidance for those seeking to navigate the complexities of the spiritual realm with authority and confidence. It's a must-read for anyone eager to unlock the fullness of divine justice and experience the liberty and blessings that rightfully belong to the children of God. An absolute masterpiece in the realm of spiritual literature!

REVIEW BY CARMEN WILDE

"Unlocking Divine Justice: Navigating the Courts of Heaven" is an extraordinary and transformative work that delves deep into the heart of spiritual intercession and divine justice. The author brilliantly navigates the intricate landscape of the spiritual realm, offering readers an unparalleled understanding of how to approach God as Father, Friend, and Judge.

The book's profound insights into the legalities of the spiritual realm are both eye-opening and deeply empowering. It sheds light on the often-unseen dynamics that can hinder prayers and block divine intervention, offering a clear and actionable path to spiritual breakthroughs. The author's thorough exploration of biblical narratives, coupled with practical guidance, makes the complex themes of spiritual warfare and intercession accessible and relatable to readers from all walks of life.

One of the most compelling aspects of this book is its emphasis on the power of addressing historical and generational spiritual issues. The practical steps towards rectifying broken covenants and dismantling legal grounds used by adversaries are invaluable, providing readers with the tools to not only understand but actively engage in spiritual battles with wisdom and authority.

Furthermore, the author's compassionate and empowering approach to guiding readers through the process of spiritual cleansing and repentance is both refreshing and deeply moving. The book doesn't just offer knowledge; it offers transformation, inviting readers to step into a life of freedom and divine alignment.

In "Unlocking Divine Justice," the reader will find a treasure of spiritual wisdom, a beacon of hope, and a guide for walking in the fullness of God's justice and blessings. This book is more than a read; it's an experience, an invitation to embark on a journey of profound spiritual awakening and empowerment. Absolutely essential for anyone looking to deepen their spiritual understanding and walk in the victorious liberty that God intends for His children. A truly remarkable and life-changing book!

www.ingramcontent.com/pod-product-compliance
Lightning Source LLC
Chambersburg PA
CBHW020258180726
47994CB00028B/3170